Inform
For Beginners

How To Create and Market Profitable Online Courses, eBooks, and Other Digital Content Online

By: Argena Olivis

www.argenaolivis.com

Bonus: Download Your Free Kindle Book Creation Course

Learn how to create and market your first kindle book online.

You can use this course to get started making money online.

Plus, when you subscribe you'll receive my best tips and tutorials for online business success.

Learn how I'm making money from the following methods: kindle publishing, affiliate marketing, email marketing, information products, blogging, and more.

Visit

http://www.argenaolivis.com/freekindlecourse/

to get your free course

Table of Contents

Introduction

I want to thank you and congratulate you for reading the book, *"Information Products For Beginners: How To Create and Market Online Courses, eBooks, and Other Digital Products Online"*

This book contains proven steps and strategies on how to create and market your first information product online.

Physical products are great, but in order to create true passive income and be able to live the freedom lifestyle, you have to sell something online that is independent of your time.

Anyone can create an information product, all you need is the knowledge of marketing and the motivation to get the product out there.

People have no problem paying for a solution. People buy information all the time. This includes: eBooks, video courses, printables, memberships, and more.

You may be wondering if you have what it takes to sell information, and the answer is yes!

You don't have to be an expert on the topic you're teaching, you just have to know more than the student. There are tons of things that you know, that people are willing to pay to learn.

Don't be afraid to sell. Free information is great, but people tend to not take action on information they get for free. But when they invest money into a product, they're more likely to take action. Sometimes customers don't take action on products they paid for too.

You have to value what you know. If you don't know much, then it's never too late to start studying and learning some new things that will increase your value.

Information products are the way of the future. Customers will always appreciate getting the information they need sent right to them instantly.

Thanks again for reading *Information Products For Beginners*, I hope you find it valuable and I'm able to walk you through the process of getting your first information product out there.

Make sure to take action on what you read, every day that you don't have anything up for sale, you're missing out on income.

Chapter 1: What Product To Create

The first thing you have to do is decide on a niche. Since your reading this book, you may already have a niche or product in mind.

The most important thing in choosing a niche is making sure it's profitable. To find out if a niche is profitable, see if other people have products in that niche already.

If there are products being sold, then people are most likely making money and customers are buying these products.

Don't worry about competition, there is plenty to go around. And if you market your product the right way to the right audience then you should do well.

Not only do you need to know your niche, but you need to know your target market. Knowing your target market will make marketing your product much easier.

Your target market is a specific group of people who would be interested in purchasing your product because it can help them, or they would desire it.

So think about it, who is your target market?

Consider the following demographics:

- women or men

- age

- ethnicity

- income level

- education level

You need to know these types of things about your audience. If you don't, you're speaking to everyone and will not sell any information products.

You have to get your product in front of the people who are willing to buy it and who care about it.

So with that being said, the product you create depends on who your target market is and how they learn best.

If your target market likes to read, consider creating a guide.

Guide

A guide is a course, but it's in the form of downloadable document. You will walk your customer through step-by-step how to do something.

You can separate your guide into downloadable pdfs for each lesson, or just have one complete eBook type file.

If there's something that's hard to explain on paper, you can link to video files or other examples within the guide.

Video Course

If your target market learns best from watching video, you can create a video course.

You would outline what lessons that would be taught in the course, and create videos for each lesson.

If you really want to go above and beyond, consider creating downloadable pdfs to go along with each video lesson, so that the customers that learn by reading can follow along.

You do not have to show your face in the videos. You can record your computer screen by using free tools like Screencast-O-Matic or Jing.

You may need to record your computer screen in order to show your customers what you're doing on the computer, if showing your customers what you're doing on the computer it's relevant to your target market and what you're teaching.

 If not, create a PowerPoint Presentation and record the screen of your computer as you go through the slides.

eBook

An eBook is sort of like a guide but the information is not as "in depth" and step-by-step.

This is because an eBook does not have to be non-fiction, you can create eBooks on anything you target market desires.

You have to option to create non-fiction eBooks, Children's books, fiction books, stories, etc.

The list goes on and on, it's up to you and what your target market likes. As more and more people discover the internet and mobile devices, physical books sales decrease and eBook sales continue to increase.

Printables

If you have a creative idea for a packaged product that customers can use to either guide them or entertain them, consider creating printables.

Printables are items customers can download and print immediately. This can be anything from games, greeting cards, tracking sheets, party packs, etc.

People love to download and print items from the comfort of their own home and not have to worry about delivery costs.

You can have a lot of success with printables if you know what your target market wants or needs.

Audios

If your target market learns by hearing, you can sell audios to them. Audios are a good way for your customer to listen to whatever you're teaching on the go.

This can include a course with lessons, or even an audio book.

Or it can be a valuable collection of interviews you've done and recorded with people having success in that niche.

These audios can also include downloadable pdfs for those that don't like to listen.

The Takeaway

So now you have an idea of the types of information products you're able to create.

Action Steps:

- find a profitable niche

- find out what your target market is

- find out what platform your target market will learn from best

- decide if you're going to create a guide, eBook, video course, printables, or audio course

- create the product

Once you decide everything, it's now time to start setting creating your information product.

This may take a few days to a few months depending on what type of product you're going to create and how much time you have.

So create the product and move on to chapter 2.

Chapter 2: Setting It Up

In chapter 1, you learned how to find a profitable niche and a target market.

Then you created your product and now it's ready to be set up.

Now that you have your product created, we now have to see how you want to set the course up so it can run smoothly and be delivered to your customers instantly after payment.

How To Deliver Your Product

You have a few options when it comes to getting your product to your customer instantly without physically having to be there.

We're going to go into your options for delivering each product type :

eBooks, Guides, or Printables

An eBook or guide is pretty easy to deliver. All you need to do is save the files in your website's back office.

You can do this by uploading the complete file

into your back office and getting the link to the product.

To set up Paypal, go to paypal.com and set up an account. Paypal allows you to send your customer to any link after they purchase your product. Send your customer to the link that gives them access to your product.

Make sure to let the customers know that they need to save the file to their computer after they gain access to it.

Paypal is free and is a very trusted form of

payment online, your customer can pay by using a card they have on file through Paypal, or just paying with their credit card without having a Paypal account at all.

Also, consider using ejunkie.com. As of now Ejunkie is only $5 a month. You can upload your file to Ejunkie, and your customer will get the product sent straight to their email after purchase.

Consider your other options too when creating an eBook or guide. You can always publish your eBook on other platforms such as Amazon Kindle or Clickbank.

If you decide to go this route, keep in mind that Amazon will charge a fee to deliver your product. But, this can be a good thing because you'll have access to their millions of customers.

Video Course or Audios

A video course takes a little more work than an eBook or Guide.

For a video course, consider setting it up on its own website. This means you'll have to buy a domain name and hosting for it.

If you don't want it on its own domain, you also have the option to use an existing website where customers can create accounts and log in to access the course they paid for.

Either way, you'll need a website. If you don't have one yet find out how to create one here: http://argenaolivis.com/website

There is a free WordPress plugin called S2Member where you can set up payment gateways so customers are only allowed to access the information they've paid for.

S2Member has great resources and videos that show you how to set everything up.

To get the course-like set up, use a free WordPress plugin called Namaste.

For video courses, there are also other platforms you can use. Udemy is a place where you can create video courses, and they are sold to their millions of students. Like Amazon, they will take a cut of your profit but it's still an option if you want to get some extra eyeballs on your product.

You also have the option to put your course on

paid platforms that will handle all the hosting and other technical support, like Kajabiapp.com.

Sales Page

Now that you have your product created and set up, it's time to create a sales page.

Make sure you have a picture of what the product looks like. You can get this outsourced for only $5 on Fiverr.com. So if you have an eBook or guide make sure to have a picture of it to put on your sales page.

For your audio or video course, you can create a

logo for the product to have on the sales page.

The sales page needs to include:

- what's included in the product

- how this product will solve your target market's problem

- how many pages, minutes, or length the product is

- a money back guarantee

- testimonials and or reviews

The sales page can be as long as you need it to be to answer all of your prospects questions or worries they'll think of before purchasing the product.

Be clear on who the product is for and who it's not for, it'll only save you time and money.

To have a high converting sales page, make sure to brush up on your copywriting skills.

Testing

Once you have your product created, set up, and your sales page up you're almost ready to go. But first, make sure everything is working right.

If you're using Paypal, make sure the buy button is working correctly. I usually test this by changing the price to $0.01 cent to make sure that payment is going through to me and I'm being delivered straight to the product.

Also, if relevant, test Ejunkie to make sure it's working correctly.

Ensure everything is running smoothly so you can start marketing your product.

The Takeaway

Now you should have your product created and set up. You're moving right along here.

Action Steps:

- decide what platform you want your product delivered

- set up payment for your product

- create a sales page

Okay, you have some work to do!

Chapter 3: Marketing The Product

Okay, so now that you have your product created and set up it's time to start marketing the product so you can start making some money.

If you already have an audience and a brand that you've been interacting with and creating free valuable content for, this part will be simple.

But, if you don't, you can still get quality customers to buy your product just as long as you market your product the right way.

One of the platforms you may consider is Clickbank.

Clickbank

Clickbank.com is a place for information products. Every day, marketers are creating products and putting them on Clickbank.

This is a smart move because there are millions of affiliates that can promote your product for you. The catch is you have to pay them a commission for getting your product out in front of their audience.

Affiliates on Clickbank like to market products that are relevant to their audience, high quality and have a high converting sales page.

They also like to deal with affiliates that have lots of support. So really help your affiliates out by offering them things like email swipes, headlines, and images of the product.

If you haven't yet, you may want to attend some internet marketing events and find some like-minded people that are interested in what you're doing and are willing to market your product to their email list.

Marketers who have a huge email list, and have built trust with that list will give your product the push it needs.

If your product is high quality you will start getting referrals and reviews.

Facebook Ads

You need to build a community of trustworthy fans to win on Facebook. Create a Facebook fan page for your business.

Your page should give away free high-quality tips, quotes, and images relevant to your target market. Update your page every hour on the hour.

Having a Facebook page is something you should do before even launching your product so you can give your fans something to look forward to.

Do your research on how to have a successful product launch so the first day your product comes out it will make a ton of sales from eager fans.

There are billions of users on Facebook, so I'm sure your target market is hanging out there.

So run some Facebook Ads to the product page, this will get you, buyers. Make sure your ads are shown to people in your target market. Facebook does a good job at narrowing down who your ads will be shown to.

Email

Build an email list by having a squeeze page that gives away a free opt-in offer. The opt-in offer should be quality and relevant to your target market.

If you don't know how to set up your email list, visit: http://www.argenaolivis.com/email-marketing-101/

Market your product to your email list. Similar to Facebook, you want to give away free quality content to your list before you sell them.

You also want to have a few emails leading up to the launch of your product.

The thing that works best when selling products

to your list is using scarcity, let them know there's a sale that's going to be ending; or that there's a bonus you're giving away with the product will be no longer be available after a certain date.

Social Media

Use popular sites like YouTube, Twitter, Google +, and Pinterest to get your product out there.

Make sure to use relevant hashtags when talking about the product on these sites.

You can post things like:

- testimonials

- a walkthrough of the product

- images of the product in action

- demonstrations

The possibilities are endless. You can also advertise on these sites. It's time you let people know about your product.

Affiliates

You don't have to go through a platform like

Clickbank to get affiliates for your product.

You can offer an affiliate program for your product on your own.

Let prospects know about the affiliate program and what it has to offer.

Make sure people can access it by having a page on your website about it.

Take your time with this, and let people know why they should become an affiliate for your product.

The Takeaway

Use multiple platforms to get your product out there. Consider using a platform like Clickbank to skyrocket your sales.

Action Steps:

- upload your product to Clickbank

- use Facebook ads to drive targeted traffic to your product

- build an email list and launch the product using scarcity

- advertise your product on large social media sites

- open an affiliate program for your product

Chapter 4: Upselling

Creating your first product was nice, but now what can you do to create more related products that can further help your customers?

No matter how much your first product costs, you can always find a way to make more money and offer your customers more value.

Having another product that is higher priced or has residual billing is called upselling.

This product is usually not introduced to the

customer until they've purchased your first one. It's a step up for them, where they can learn more or do more with another product.

You have a few options. You can make higher priced products that relate to your first one. Or you can create a group or coaching that in order to be a part of, customers would be charged a monthly fee.

Creating Complimentary Products

The next product you create should feed off of the product you already have. This means it should be similar, but it should offer a lot more information or access to others who will help them.

Or, if the product you've created "has it all", consider creating a product for a lower price that doesn't have as much information.

Pricing Products

Many internet marketers have lower priced products that upsell the higher priced items.

This is a great thing because if the lower priced product is valuable, then the customers can expect the rest of the products to be quality as well.

Here is a great pricing structure:

Product #1: $7

Product #2: $27

Product #3: $47

Product #4: 67

And so on. Keep in mind that you can go straight from $7 to $67, do not underestimate your product's value.

Price your product at what you think its worth.

But make sure to over deliver and do your best.

Bonuses

Create bonuses for your product. These bonuses can be as simple as an extra video or an eBook.

You can have it so customers can buy the product, or they can buy the product and the bonus at the same time for more money.

Bonuses are good for launching. You can offer a limited time bonus they can get but for only a limited time. After that take the bonus off the table.

Types of bonuses you can create:

- eBook

- guide

- audio files

- videos

- printables

- coaching

- access to a mastermind group

- discount

Bonuses are also a great way to upsell. Add bonuses into your sales funnel and watch your product sales increase.

Chapter 5: Returns and Customer Service

If you offer a money back grantee to your customers, you have to honor it.

Keep in mind that it's your product and you can do what you want with it.

You don't have to offer a money back guarantee at all, you can say that all sales are final.

But having a money back guarantee increases sales and trust with customers.

If your product is super high quality and exceeds

their expectations, you may never have to worry about returns.

But if it's not what they were looking for, you may get a few.

It's bound to happen.

Once they return the product, they will not have access to it anymore.

You have to decide rather you want the person to explain why they want to return your product, or rather you will allow returns with no questions asked.

On top of returns, you may have customers that experience errors in receiving the product or other errors.

It's the internet, and sometimes things just don't work right. So you want to have a system where they can contact you if anything goes wrong.

Ticket System

Find a ticket system that customers can use to contact you or your customer service team in order to report a problem or tell you they want a refund.

This is automated so that you don't have to worry about rushing and getting to a computer soon as something goes wrong.

The ticket system will put them at ease by sending them an email that states their request had been received and will be answered as soon as possible.

I do recommend you get back to your customers in a timely manner, because that's just good customer service.

VA

Consider hiring a part-time virtual assistant to handle customer care. This assistant will be on call at all times and you'll never have to hear about a problem with the product.

If you truly want a freedom lifestyle, a VA will be necessary. But depending on your situation, you may want to make sure you're making enough money to pay the VA first.

So at one point you may be doing all the

customer service, but no worries, you'll figure it out.

Dealing With Negative Feedback

Rather it's a review or just people complaining about your product, don't look at it as a failure and don't let it get to you.

You have to decide rather the feedback is constructive or just someone being an idiot, which will happen.

Use all the constructive criticism to make your

product better.

Tell your customers when you've made an update to the product. They will appreciate your efforts.

The Takeaway

As long as you have a quality product and are giving your customers outstanding customer service you should be fine.

Don't worry too much about returns unless you know you've under delivered.

Make sure your sales page tells the customer exactly what to expect.

Don't be hard on yourself, use negative feedback on your product as a way to improve it.

Take Action:

- develop a ticket system

- improve your product based on the feedback

- consider hiring a VA to deal with customers

Chapter 6: Time To Take Action

You now have everything you need to know to create your information product. Keep in mind that you don't have to be an expert. Be knowledgeable about the product you're creating by doing proper research.

Lead people in the right direction and truly help people. It's great to make money, but it's awesome to change lives by providing value.

Don't feel bad for selling, selling helps people

take action. Many people do not value free information because there's so much of it out there on the internet today.

Personal Development

You're obviously in business. Try to become the best you that you can be for yourself, your family, and your customers.

Read inspirational books and business books that will better your life.

Set goals so you can one day accomplish the lifestyle you desire.

Challenge yourself by creating 30-day challenges each month.

Hustle every day until you reach financial freedom.

Finding Time

I don't know your situation, but creating a product is going to take time.

I know you may be busy, but if you truly want this, you'll find time.

Wake up earlier, or go to sleep later. This will all be worth it in the end.

Whatever time you have, make sure you're taking focused action. Take all the action steps in this book and you'll do just fine.

Mindset

You have to have the right mindset in order to create something great. Believe in yourself and in your product.

Whatever you do, do it with excellence.

Have an entrepreneur mindset for success.

Watch who your friends are and what you're

exposing your mind to.

You may want to turn off the T.V. And start

watching business YouTube videos. And you

may want to turn off the music and start

listening to business podcasts.

Whatever you decide, I know you'll do great!

Conclusion

Thank you again for reading *Information Products For Beginners*!

I hope this book was able to help you to create an information product.

The next step is to go back to Chapter 1 and take the action steps needed.

Finally, if you enjoyed this book, then I'd like to ask you for a favor, would you be kind enough to leave a review for this book on Amazon? It'd be greatly appreciated!

Your review will help others to find the book, and it'll also give me feedback on what I can improve or what I did well.

Thank you and good luck!

Preview of 'How To Make Money Online Fast'

Chapter 1: Kindle Publishing

Wow, where do I begin? You should know that I started my online journey in 2012. I was in college and looking for a way to make some extra money online.

That's when I came across website creation. While researching how to create a website on YouTube I was shocked to find that there were people making tons of money online.

That's when I started going from "I want to

make money online" to "I want to create an online business."

As the story goes, I started reading business books, buying courses, and of course building websites.

Many of the websites I built failed and never made a profit. Then everything changed, I decided I didn't want to work a job, I wanted to be an entrepreneur full time.

So I started to really focus on making an income online. I purchased two courses that then changed my life.

I started taking massive action and, now I'm here, making a decent income online and writing this book to you-- the person who also has dreams of making their first dollar online.

Believe me, this stuff really works. You just have to change your mindset and really do the work.

None of these strategies work without work. You may find yourself up late and up early, or sacrificing your TV time to try to make this work.

Whatever you do, if you truly want to make it you have to put in the time and you have to want it bad enough.

I found that Kindle Publishing by far the simplest method of making money online. This is because Amazon is the number one website that people shop.

So if you know what you're doing, you can truly clean up on Amazon.

How To Create A Kindle Book

The "how to" of creating a kindle book is pretty simple; optimizing it so that it can be found as the harder part.

Yes, Amazon has a lot of customers, but it also has a lot of authors. More and more people are publishing Kindle books every single day and every day the marketplace is becoming more saturated.

It's one of those things where you better get in when you can.

Step 1: Decide what market or niche that you want to write your book in. You have options to write nonfiction books, fiction books, erotica, and children's books.

It should be a niche you're familiar with. If you do decide to write a book in a niche you're not familiar with, make sure to do the proper research in order to create a quality book.

It's important that the niche that you write your book in is profitable.

If you decide to write a nonfiction book, look up the keyword that you want to target in the Amazon Kindle store. If you see books on the first page for the keyword and has rank under 100,000 then it's a profitable niche.

Typically books with an Amazon sales rank lower than 100,000 are making $30+ a month.

Step 2: Create a title for your book. When writing a nonfiction book use the keywords from the niche you've chosen. Your title should have relevant keywords in it so it can be found easily in the kindle store.

Step 3: Open up a writing document of your choice and type out your book.

Depending on how familiar you are with the subject, you can finish your book in a day. I typically try to write for 2 hours a day, so I can finish books in about 3-7 days.

If you're writing a children's book you will have to hire an illustrator. You can find low priced illustrators by going to www.fiverr.com.

Your book does not have to be long, but it does have to be quality if you truly want to make sales. Bad reviews can slow down or eliminate your sales.

Unless it's a children's book, your book should be 15 or more pages.

You can find a template online by Googling kindle templates if you want to use a template to guide your writing.

Your nonfiction book should include an introduction, 4-6 chapters, and a conclusion.

Step 4: Upload your book to KDP. Go to www.kdp.amazon.com and if you haven't done so yet, open up a KDP account.

Add all the necessary information into KDP. The whole process is pretty self-explanatory, so you'll be able to enter the necessary information.

Step 5: Design your cover using the Kindle Cover Creator. The Kindle Cover Creator is a free software by Amazon that you can use to create your book covers. They give you free templates, it's really cool.

If you're creative and design well, this too will be very beneficial to you. If not, I suggest going to www.fiverr.com and ordering your cover for only $5.

Then you're finished. The process gets easier as you continue to create more and more books.

If your book is not selling, consider this:

- the niche may be too competitive

- you're not using the correct keywords

- you have a lot of bad reviews

- your cover is not attractive enough

- your book is not in the correct categories or the categories are too competitive

There are many factors that go into rather or not your book sells. Make sure you enroll your book in the KDP select program in order to have a free promotion for your book.

These free promotions are for 5 days every three months. When a lot of people download your book it will help your book rank for its keywords.

So now the thing to do is take action! Use this guide and start creating your kindle book today.

The sooner you get it up, the faster you make money online!

Discover more ways to promote your kindle book by taking my video course on how to create and market your first kindle book: http://www.argenaolivis.com/freekindlecourse

Visit *www.ArgenaOlivis.com* to continue reading How To Make Money Online

Or go to: **http://amzn.to/1qNSJNs**

Check Out My Other Books

Below you'll find some of my other popular books that are popular on Amazon and Kindle as well. Alternatively, you can visit my author page on Amazon to see other work done by me.

How To Make Money Online Fast: Step By Step Instructions On How To Work From Home Using Proven Internet Marketing Strategies

Affiliate Marketing 101: How To Make Money Online With Other People's Products

Email Marketing Machine: Build Relationships, Traffic, and Make Money Online

Kindle Publishing Back End: Guide To Creating A Real Business With Kindle Publishing

Bonus: Download Your Free Kindle Book Creation Course

Learn how to create and market your first kindle book online.

You can use this course to get started making money online.

Plus, when you subscribe you'll receive my best tips and tutorials for online business success.

Learn how I'm making money from the following methods: kindle publishing, affiliate marketing, email marketing, information products, blogging, and more.

Visit

http://www.argenaolivis.com/freekindlecourse/

to get your free course

Made in the USA
Columbia, SC
30 May 2018